Building Your Website

with Thrive Themes and Plugins

Book 6 in the Internet Marketing FAST series

Copyright and Enquiries

Contents

Building Your Website

with Thrive Themes and Plugins

Building Your Website

with Thrive Themes and Plugins

Table of Figures

Building Your Website

with Thrive Themes and Plugins

Building Your Website

with Thrive Themes and Plugins

Thrive: Themes and Plugins I Wouldn't be Without

Figure 1: Thrive Themes

WordPress is arguably the best, easiest and most effective platform to build a commercial website on.

But much of its strength comes from the huge number of themes and plugins that have been created to extend its functionality. Some are free. Many are not. They don't all co-exist peacefully. Some used to be good, but haven't been updated to work with later versions of WordPress.

Building Your Website

It can be a bit of a minefield.

Thrive Themes and Plugins are a set of conversion optimized themes and plugins that do away with the need for anything else. They work seamlessly with WordPress and with each other and are frequently updated. Thrive University provides in-depth training via text and video.

I've been a user of Thrive Themes and Plugins for years and simply would not attempt to build a website without them. They are exactly what you need to build customer-focused, income-producing websites.

Affiliate Disclaimer: After using them for years, I recently decided to promote them officially as an affiliate. This means that if you buy Thrive Themes through my link, I get paid a commission. You are charged exactly the same amount, so there is no downside to you. The upside is that you will get all of my training on the best ways to use the Thrive themes and the Thrive plugins for free.

Thrive Themes is sold as a membership. For a single membership payment, you get

- Access to the full suite of Thrive WordPress plugins
- A beautiful set of eye-catching WordPress themes
- Constant updates and access to new plugins
- Thrive University
- Autoresponder integration
- Exclusive members only courses, templates and content
- Unlimited support.

Building Your Website

with Thrive Themes and Plugins

What Does It Cost?

Thrive membership costs $199 per quarter or $499 per year and this entitles you to use all of the themes and plugins on up to 5 websites.

There is a 30-day money-back guarantee.

To purchase Thrive Themes or simply to investigate further, please click:

THRIVE THEMES AND PLUGINS

Installation

Thrive makes it very easy to install their themes and plugins.

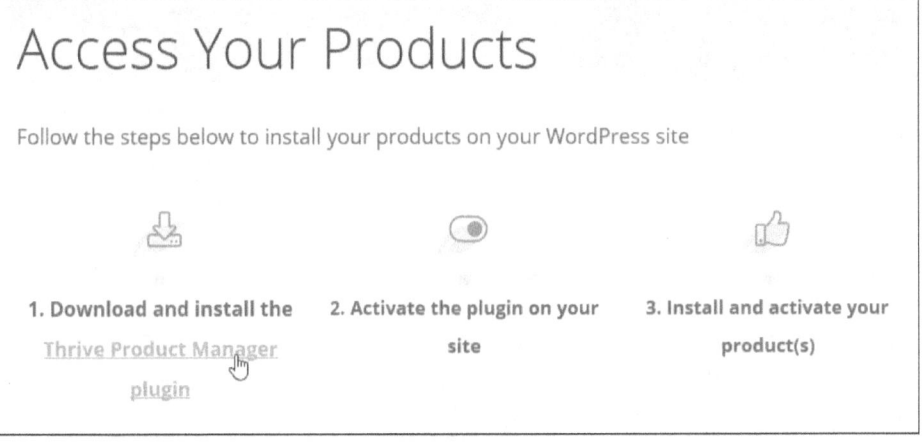

Figure 2: Install Thrive Product Manager

You only need one plugin. It's called thrive-product-manager.zip and you'll be given access to it when you purchase Thrive Themes. Install it as you would any other plugin.

It allows you to install any or all of the Thrive Themes and Plugins.

Building Your Website

with Thrive Themes and Plugins

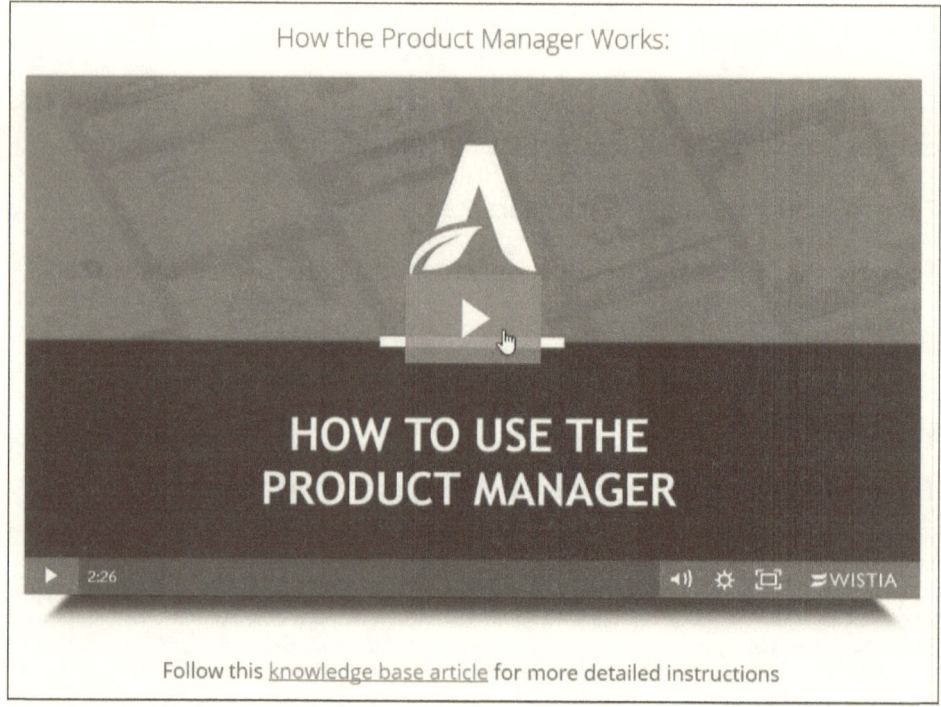

Figure 3: Thrive Product Manager Video

There's even a video explaining how to install and use the plugin.

Click on *Product Manager* in the main WP Menu and then log in to Thrive Themes with the username and password you created when you purchased.

Building Your Website

with Thrive Themes and Plugins

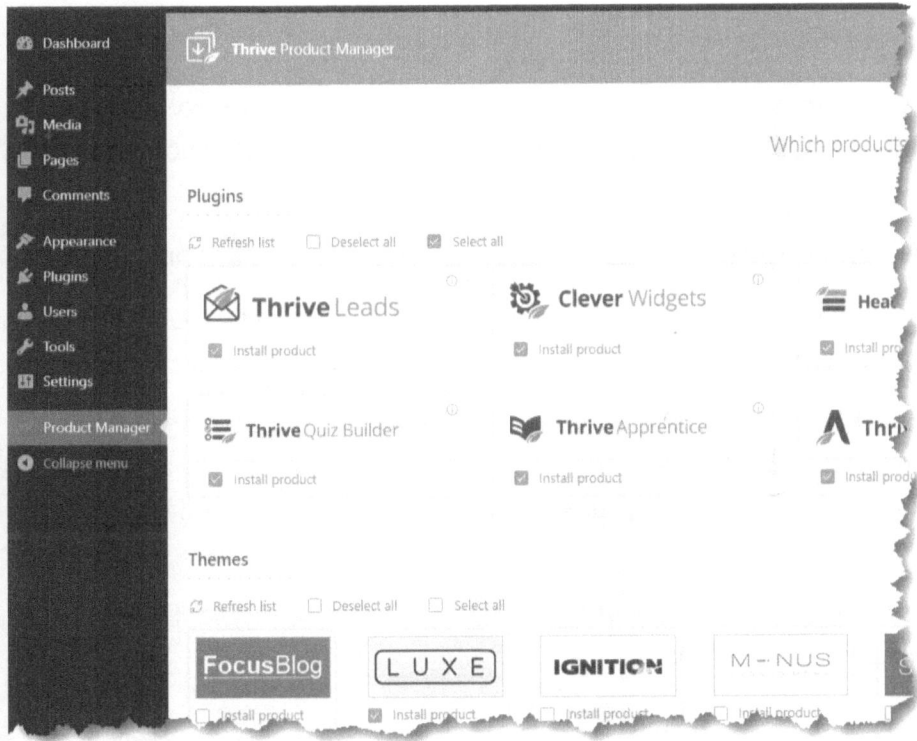

Figure 4: Select the Plugins and Themes to Install

You are shown all of the Thrive plugins and themes that are available.

Select the ones you want to install and click *Install Selected Products*.

You don't need to install everything at once. You can come back any time you want and install more.

Install the Thrive Theme Builder and Thrive Architect

Here is a summary of what you get.

Building Your Website

with Thrive Themes and Plugins

Thrive Themes

Thrive comes with a theme builder that allows you to control every aspect of your site's theme, including headers, footers, menus, colors, fonts and so on.

Just work through the wizard, selecting from the many options available.

You can go back and make changes any time you like, so feel free to experiment.

Any change you make is reflected globally throughout your site. For example, if you changed the font size and color for your h1 heading setting. all your h1 headings on your site would be immediately updated. This is a huge time saver.

Here are some of my websites that were built with the Thrive Theme Builder:

https://agingslowdown.com/

https://dogmastertraining.com/

https://happyfitandslim.com/

https://imfasttraining.com/

https://superaffiliatechallenge.com/

https://thebookinside.com/

https://thescamwarrior.com/

Building Your Website

with Thrive Themes and Plugins

Connect to Autoresponder

Setting up your MailChimp or ActiveCampaign autoresponder is covered in Book 13 in the IM FAST Series: *Building Your Mailing List*, but I'm including the connection process here in case you already have one set up.

I've recommended MailChimp for years, despite their clunky interface.

Why?

Because they had the best FREE offer available.

Note "HAD".

As a free member, you could take advantage of most of their facilities except for support, until you had a substantial number of subscribers, when you could presumably afford to upgrade.

To me, that was a great business model and it made MailChimp very successful.

Though their deliverability was always a little suspect.

But then they started removing features from the free version.

First to go was the ability to have more than one mailing list. Not as drastic as it sounds. You can have one big list, segmented by groups and tags. Still...

But then, the latest change totally removed automations. The ability to create a follow-up series of emails after someone opts-in to your list. Now you can send one email, but that's it.

Wha? This is the reason you have an auto-responder.

So it's bye bye MailChimp.

Building Your Website

with Thrive Themes and Plugins

I'm sorry to recommend a paid platform instead of a free one, but it's just so much better.

ActiveCampaign is a fabulous solution at $59 per month (or $43.50 per month if paid yearly). Its automation feature, which shows a visual flow chart of where all your contacts are at in your email series, is the clearest tool I've ever seen. Everything about its user interface is top class.

Building Your Website

with Thrive Themes and Plugins

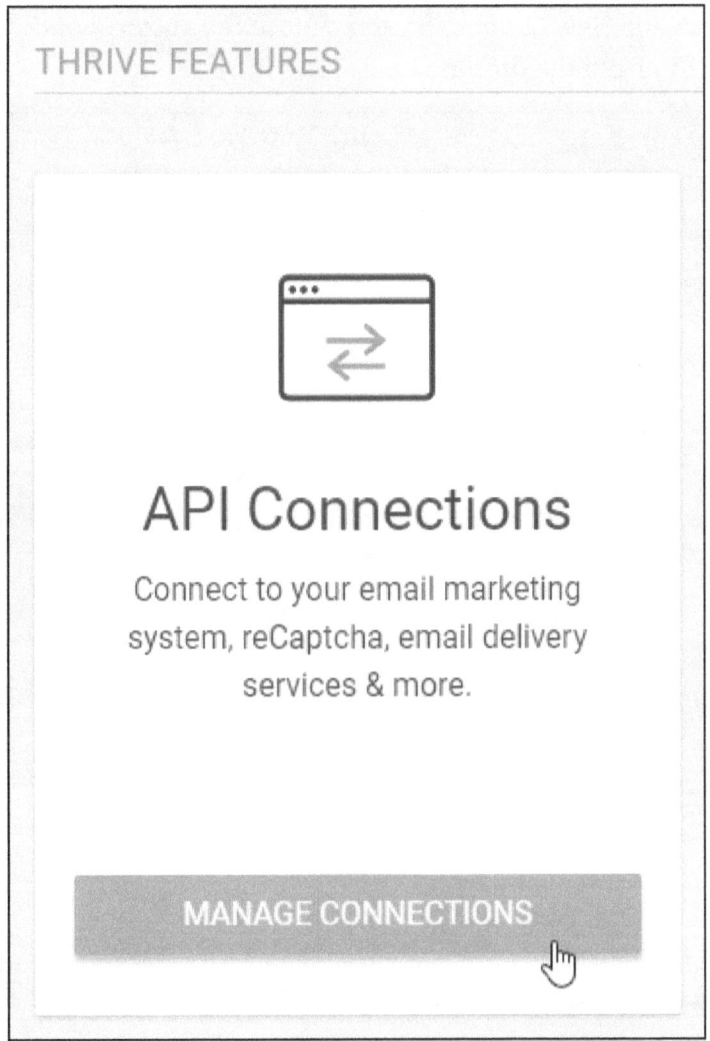

Figure 5: Thrive Dashboard API Connections

In the left-hand WP menu, go to Thrive Dashboard and under *API Connections*, select *Manage Connections*.

Building Your Website

Then select Add New Connection and choose the autoresponder you wish to connect to from the drop-down list.

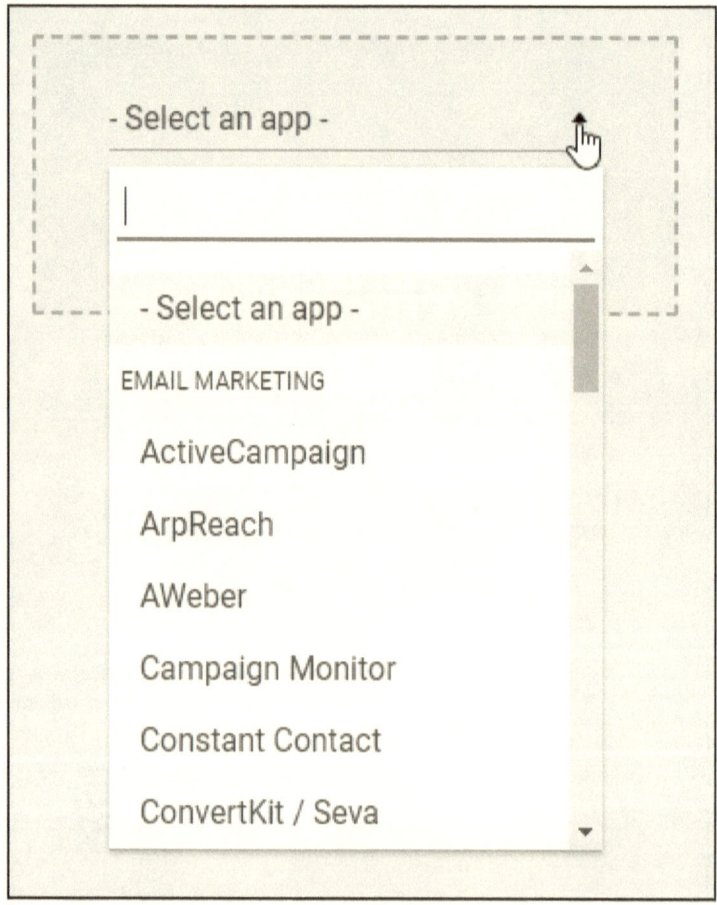

Figure 6: Select the App to Connect

Then enter your autoresponder's API key. You obtain this from your auto-responder account details.

Building Your Website

with Thrive Themes and Plugins

ACTIVE CONNECTIONS

Mailchimp

Notification: If you would like to use Transactional emails. You should fill in the Mandrill API Key and Mandrill-approved email address optional fields.

API key

☐ Add Mandrill Connection

CANCEL   CONNECT

BACK TO DASHBOARD

Building Your Website

with Thrive Themes and Plugins

Figure 7: Enter the Autoresponder's API Key

Click *Connect* and you're done.

Figure 8: Autoresponder Connection Active

If you don't currently have an autoresponder, this will all make sense after you read Book 13 in the IM FAST Series: *Building Your Mailing List*.

Building Your Website

with Thrive Themes and Plugins

Thrive Plugins

Here is a list of the 10 Thrive plugins.

Thrive Architect

Thrive Optimize

Thrive Leads

Thrive Quiz Builder

Thrive Ultimatum

Thrive Ovation

Clever Widgets

Headline Optimizer

Thrive Apprentice

Thrive Comments

Thrive Architect is covered next. The others are covered in the *Internet Marketing FAST* user guides *The Thrive Expert*.

Building Your Website

with Thrive Themes and Plugins

Thrive Architect

Figure 9: Thrive Architect

Purpose: Thrive Architect is hands-down the best WordPress editor available. It completely replaces both the WordPress classic editor and the new but clunky Gutenberg. In my opinion, Thrive Architect by itself is worth the price of Thrive Themes. What you see is what you get: drag and drop your way to pages and posts that look exactly the way you want. Build your pages in real time straight from within the editor. The Thrive Optimize add-on allows you to split test landing page variations against each other automatically.

Building Your Website

with Thrive Themes and Plugins

Here is a step by step guide to using Thrive Architect at a basic level.

Thrive Architect: Basic

Adding a New Post

Let's look at adding a new post to our website. We will use Thrive Architect to build the post, using headings, text, images and the More... tag. And we'll see how an element called Post Grid can build an attractive page that showcases all of our articles automatically.

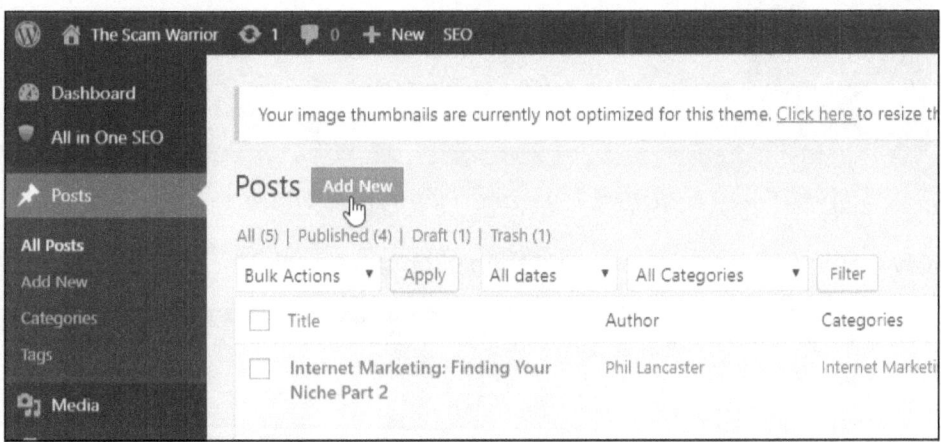

Figure 10: Add New Post in WordPress

Start off by adding a new post to your WordPress site.

Building Your Website

with Thrive Themes and Plugins

Launch Thrive Architect

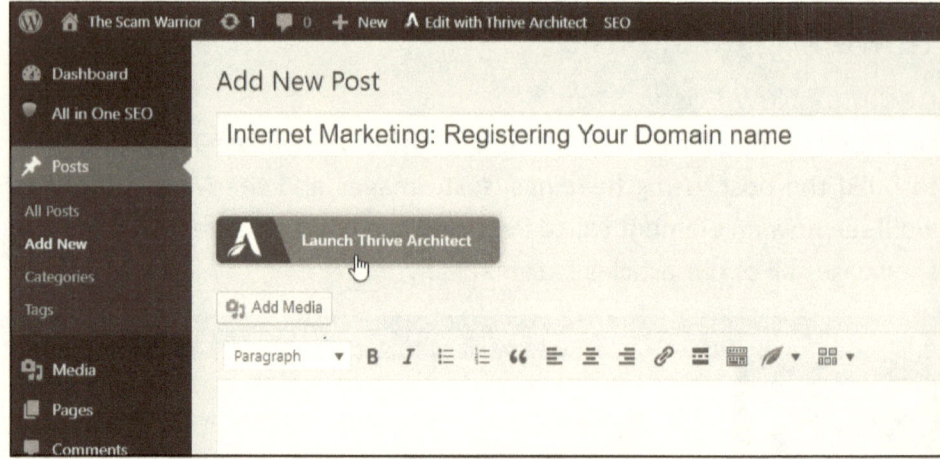

Figure 11: Launch Thrive Architect

Give your new post a name and then click on *Launch Thrive Architect*.

Figure 12: Thrive Architect Empty Page

You will then see your empty blog post inside Thrive Architect.

Building Your Website

It's divided into three sections.

The middle section shows what the post looks like. It's totally what you see is what you get.

The left-hand section shows details of the currently selected element. There are no elements on the post yet.

Selecting an Element

The right-hand section shows a + symbol that you use to select elements to drag and drop onto the page and a gear symbol with advanced options that we will cover later.

Building Your Website

with Thrive Themes and Plugins

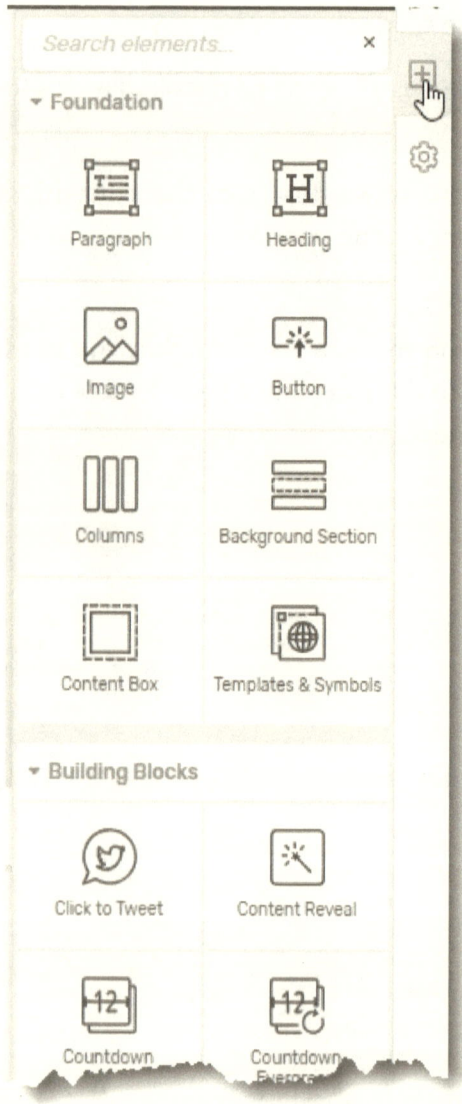

Figure 13: Thrive Architect Elements

Building Your Website

with Thrive Themes and Plugins

Although there are some 42 elements to choose from, we are going to use only Paragraph, Heading, Image and the More... tag in this user guide. There are separate guides for the others.

Note that if you just click on an element, it will appear on the post in the next available location. If you want it to appear somewhere else, simply click and drag it to the desired location.

The Text Element (Used for a Heading)

We'll start with a heading.

Click on the Text element.

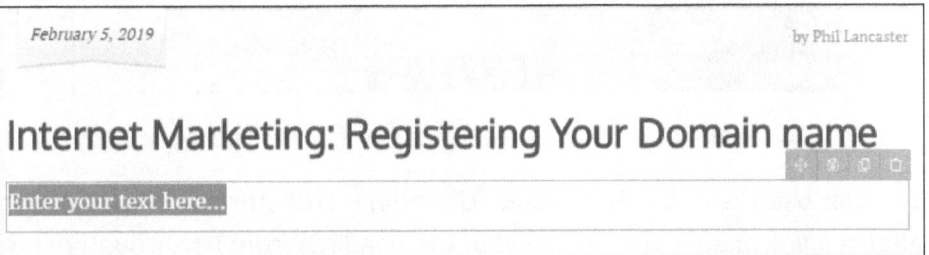

February 5, 2019   by Phil Lancaster

Internet Marketing: Registering Your Domain name

Enter your text here...

Figure 14: Select the Text Element to Create a Heading

You can enter your first heading here just by overtyping the default, which has already been selected and highlighted for you. At any time, you can preview what your post will look like on a computer monitor, tablet or phone by clicking on the corresponding symbol at the bottom of the screen.

At the top of the screen there is a handy little set of text effects.

Building Your Website

with Thrive Themes and Plugins

Figure 15: Thrive Architect Text Effects

You can use these for Bold, Italic, Underline, strikethrough, justification, adding a link or selecting the level of the heading, from h1 through to h6.

We'll select h1 for the heading and then click on the Image element on the right-hand side of the page.

Building Your Website

with Thrive Themes and Plugins

The Image Element

February 4, 2019   by Phil Lancaster

Internet Marketing: Registering Your Domain name

Your Domain Name is Your Business Address

Figure 16: Using the Image Element

Click on Insert Image to be taken to your WordPress Media Library. If you've already uploaded your image, select it there. Otherwise, click on the Upload Files tab, then Select Files and navigate to the folder containing the image you want.

Double click on it to upload it to your Media Library.

Building Your Website

with Thrive Themes and Plugins

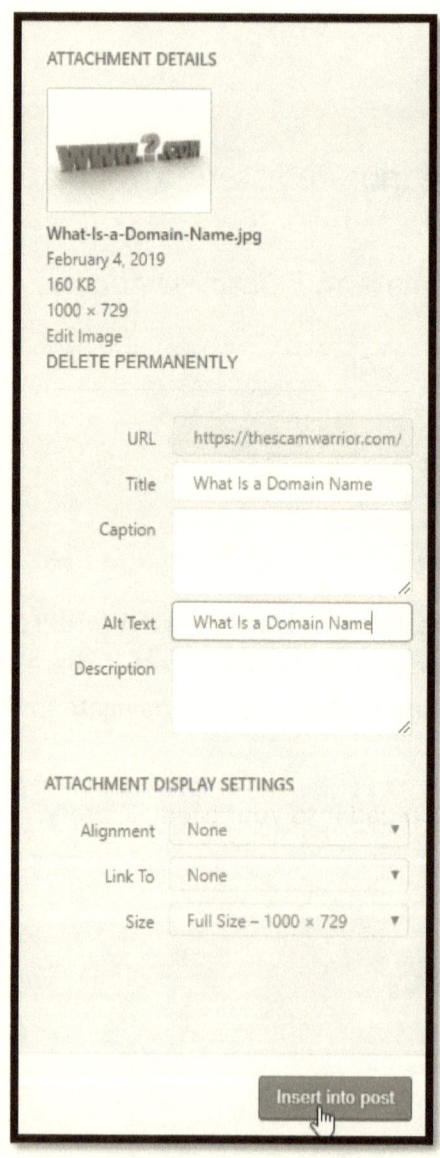

Figure 17: Getting the Image Ready

Building Your Website

The title will default to the name of the image file. You can change it here if you wish. For example, you might want to include a key word. When you're happy with the title, copy it to Alt Text so that it can be seen by search engines.

Then click *Insert into post*.

Internet Marketing: Registering Your Domain name

Your Domain Name is Your Business Address

Figure 18: Selected Image Appears on Page

The selected image appears on the page, exactly as it will appear in the blog post.

On the left-hand side, there are controls that you can use to manipulate the image.

Building Your Website

with Thrive Themes and Plugins

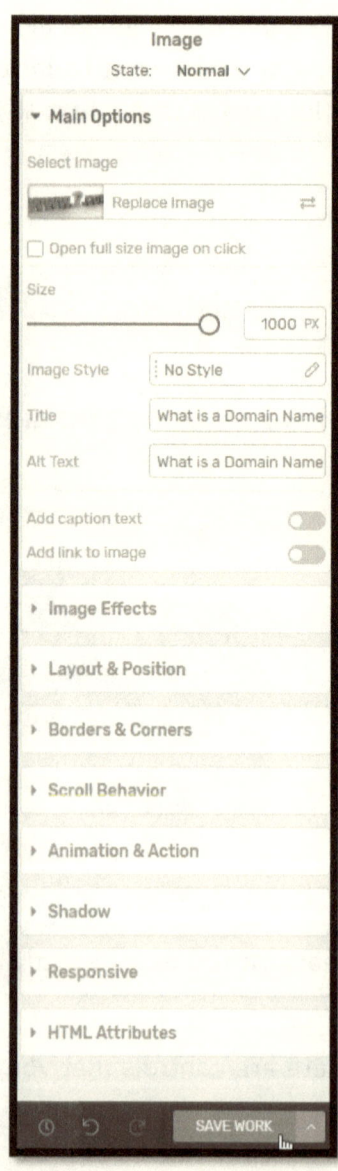

Figure 19: Image Element Controls

Building Your Website

For now, we'll leave the image as is. Later, we'll import another image, change its size and make the text flow around it. Click on *SAVE WORK*.

The Text Element (Used for a Paragraph)

Now it's time to create our first paragraph.

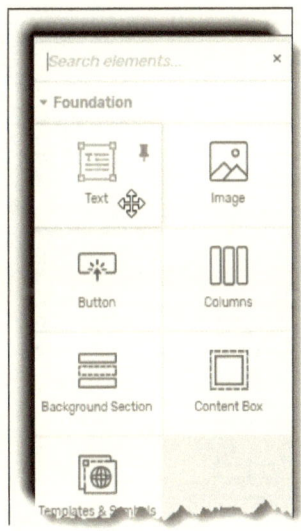

Figure 20: Select the Text Element to Create a Paragraph

The text element appears, defaulted to paragraph format and you can enter your text.

Figure 21: Enter Your Text into the Paragraph Element

Building Your Website

with Thrive Themes and Plugins

Enter your paragraph of text. Don't forget that you can format the text from the control panel at the top of the screen with effects such as bold, italic and links.

You can have multiple paragraphs.

The Content Box Element

Figure 22: Content Box Element

The Content Box element is very useful when you want to manipulate the size and position of other basic elements, such as headings, paragraphs and images.

Building Your Website

You simply put all of them inside a content box.

Then you can resize, move and position the content box as needed and all the elements inside it will be affected.

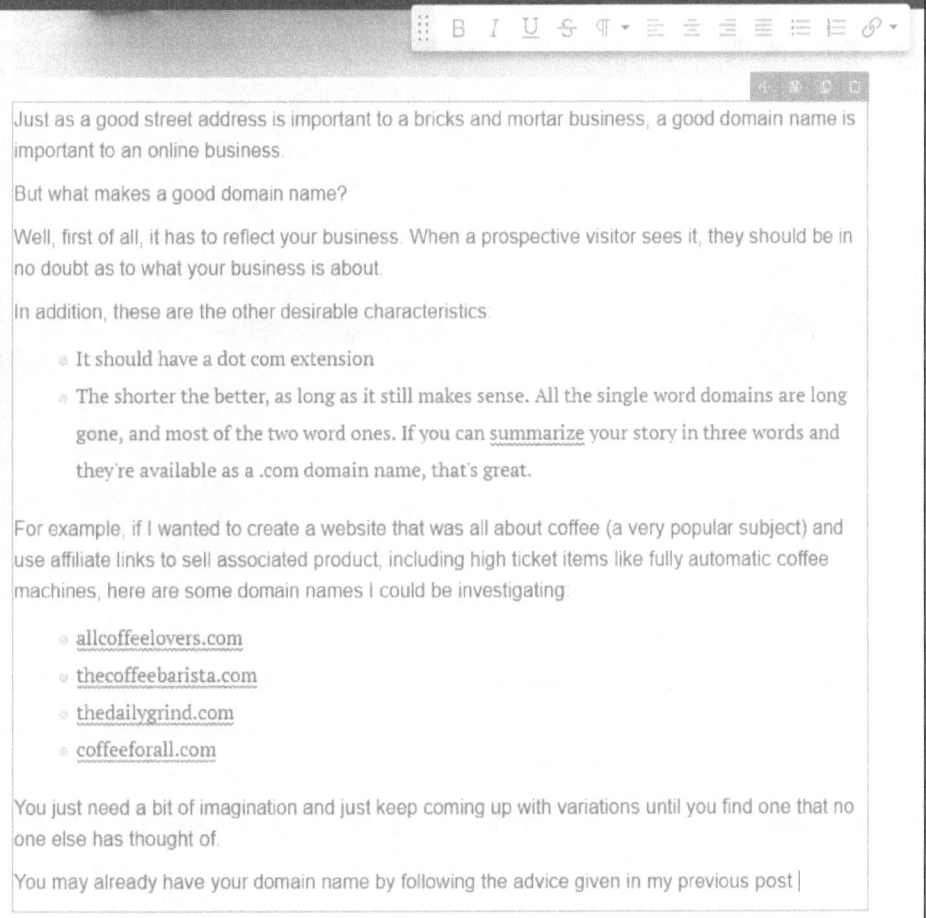

Figure 23: The Almost Complete Paragraph

Building Your Website

with Thrive Themes and Plugins

Inserting a Link

We are going to insert a link to a previous post and with Thrive Architect this is very easy.

Start by clicking the link icon in the set of controls above the paragraph.

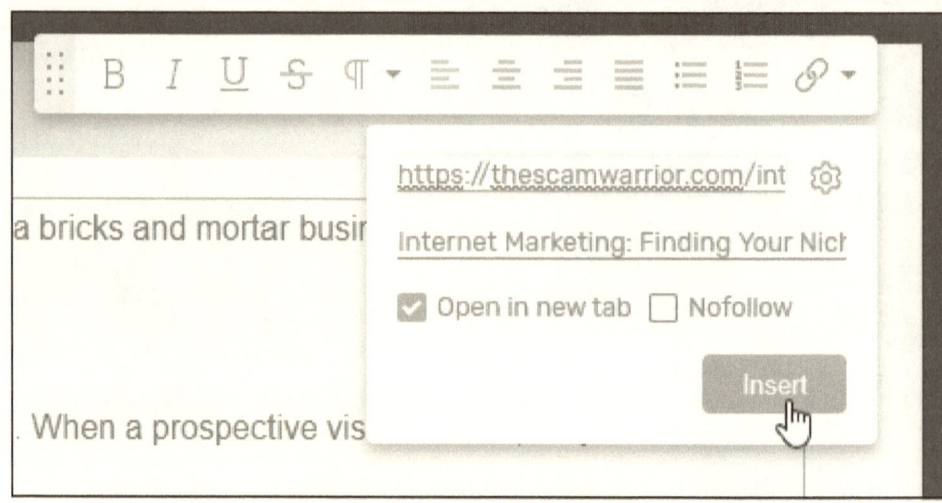

Figure 24: Inserting a Link

In this case, we are inserting a link to an existing blog post, so all you have to do is enter the first few letters of the post's name. Thrive Architect will find all matching posts. Select the one you want and it will display both the URL and the text. Both are editable.

Choose whether you want the link to open the post in a new tab or not.

Click on *Insert*.

Building Your Website

> You just need a bit of imagination and just keep coming up with variations until you find one that no one else has thought of.
>
> You may already have your domain name by following the advice given in my previous post Internet Marketing: Finding Your Niche Part 2.

Figure 25: The Link Has Been Inserted

The link has been inserted as a properly underlined link. Clicking on it will open the referenced blog post in a new tab.

Wrapping Text Around an Image

Our next section will comprise a new heading and a paragraph where the text is wrapped around an image.

This looks really professional and is easy to do.

Start off by entering the new heading, followed by the image.

Building Your Website

with Thrive Themes and Plugins

You may already have your domain name by following the advice given in my previous post <u>Internet Marketing: Finding Your Niche Part 2</u>.

What Are All These <u>TLDs</u> (Top Level domains?)

Figure 26: New Heading and Image Inserted

Next, we are going to change the size of the image so that the text can wrap around it.

Thrive Architect makes this trivially easy.

Building Your Website

with Thrive Themes and Plugins

Figure 27: Changing the Image Properties

Building Your Website

Select the image in your post. You will see the Image Properties on the left-hand side.

Move the Size slider bar to make room for the text. Don't worry about getting this exactly right. You'll still be able to move it when the text is in place and watch it flow around the image until you're totally satisfied.

To make that happen, perform the following steps:

1. Click the dropdown next to Layout and Position.

Building Your Website

with Thrive Themes and Plugins

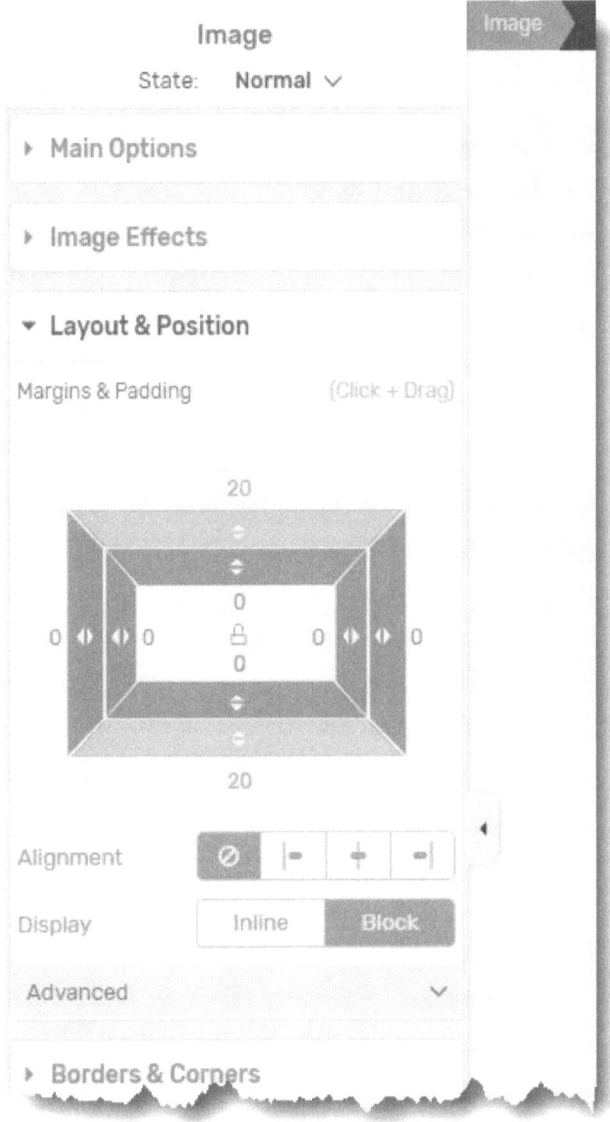

Figure 28: Image Layout and Position

Building Your Website

2. Assuming the image will be to the left and the text to the right, change the top margin to 10, the right margin to 20 and the bottom margin to 0.
3. Click on the left alignment symbol.
4. Click on the Advanced dropdown.

Building Your Website

with Thrive Themes and Plugins

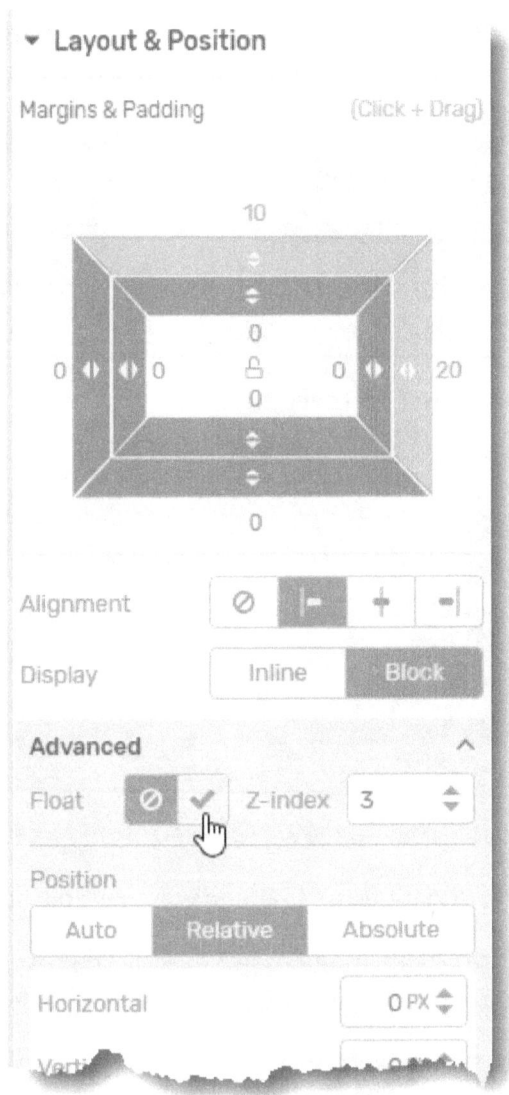

Figure 29: Change Margins and Alignment

5. Then click on the tick icon next to Float.

Building Your Website

These changes will cause the next paragraph to wrap around the image, level with the image at the top and with a 20 px space to the left, between the text and the image.

Now select a paragraph element.

Note that if you are retrofitting this to an earlier image, you make the above changes to the image properties and then click and drag the paragraph element to below the image.

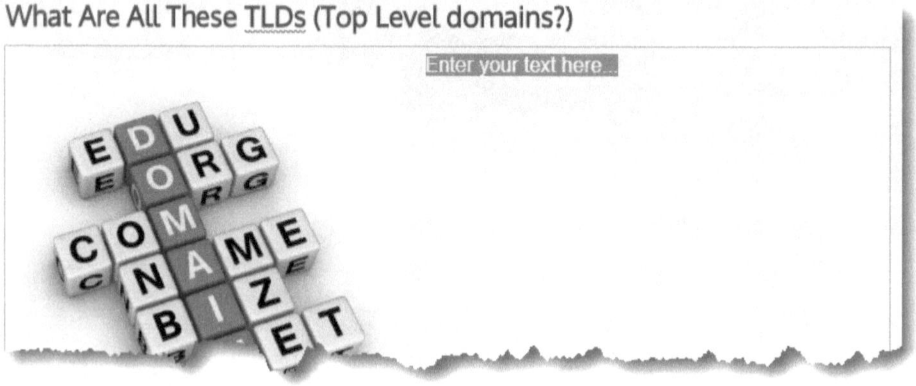

What Are All These TLDs (Top Level domains?)

Enter your text here...

Figure 30: The Text Will Flow Around the Image

Now simply enter your paragraph text and watch it flow around the image.

You can alter the size of the image to get exactly the result you want.

Building Your Website

with Thrive Themes and Plugins

What Are All These TLDs (Top Level domains?)

TLDs (Top Level Domains) are what appears to the right of the dot in your domain name.

The name you've chosen, that appears to the left of the dot, is called an SLD (Second Level Domain).

Originally, there were just three.

.com was for commercial websites like yours.

.org was for non-profit or charitable websites.

.net was for everything else on the internet. Then .info was added for sites designed to inform and educate.

Since then, there have been a proliferation of TLDs, such as .biz, .pro, .tv and so on, with new ones being constantly added. This has happened partly because of the explosion of websites, to make more possibilities available, but also simply because the more available, the more potential profit there is for the domain name registrars.

However, this has also resulted in the .com version becoming more and more valuable and highly regarded.

The upshot is simply this. Get a .com domain for your website.

Figure 31: Image and Text Wrapped

The illustration above shows the final result, with the text nicely wrapped around the image.

Performance Hint: Once you've found an image size that you like (I use a width of 400 px) it's a great idea to resize them BEFORE uploading them to WordPress media. Then you don't have to play around with the size, you have a consistent look, and your images load as fast as possible.

Building Your Website

Now complete the post with heading, paragraph and optionally new image elements.

Insert the More tag

It's generally better to show the first paragraph or so of your last few blog posts on your front page, rather than just the last post in its (scrollable) entirety.

To do that, you insert the More tag where you want to divide the post.

Everything before the tag is displayed, followed by clickable text or button to read the rest of the article.

Building Your Website

with Thrive Themes and Plugins

Figure 32: The More Tag

Building Your Website

The More tag is about half way down the elements, in the *Building Blocks* section.

Click and drag it to where you want the split to occur.

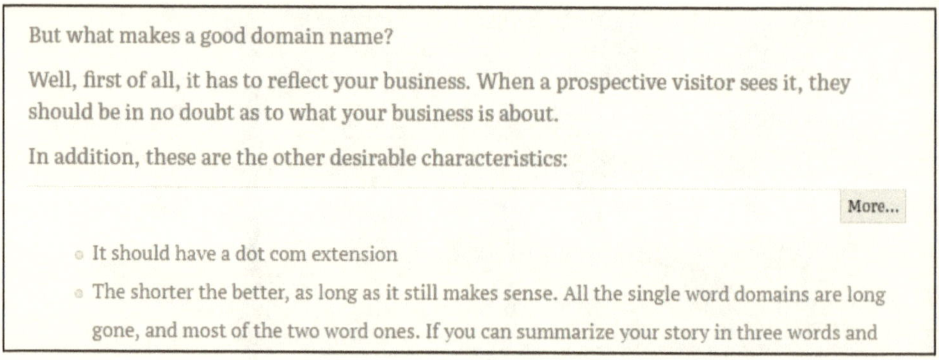

But what makes a good domain name?

Well, first of all, it has to reflect your business. When a prospective visitor sees it, they should be in no doubt as to what your business is about.

In addition, these are the other desirable characteristics:

More...

○ It should have a dot com extension

○ The shorter the better, as long as it still makes sense. All the single word domains are long gone, and most of the two word ones. If you can summarize your story in three words and

---

Figure 33: Positioning the More Tag

Publish Your New Post

Save the post in Thrive Architect, then close the window.

Back in Wordpress, click on the post name, and complete each of the following:

- Categories
- Tags
- Featured Image and
- If you have the All-in-One SEO Pack, title and description.

Then click Publish.

Building Your Website

with Thrive Themes and Plugins

February 5, 2019   by Phil Lancaster

Internet Marketing: Registering Your Domain name

Your Domain Name is Your Business Address

Just as a good street address is important to a bricks and mortar business, a good domain name is important to an online business.

But what makes a good domain name?

Well, first of all, it has to reflect your business. When a prospective visitor sees it, they should be in no doubt as to what your business is about.

In addition, these are the other desirable characteristics:

Continue reading

Figure 34: Your New Blog Post

View Your Post on Different Devices

At the very bottom of the screen, there is a preview section.

This allows you to see what your post will look like displayed on a computer monitor, a tablet or a smart phone.

Building Your Website

with Thrive Themes and Plugins

The image is scrollable, exactly as it would be on the device.

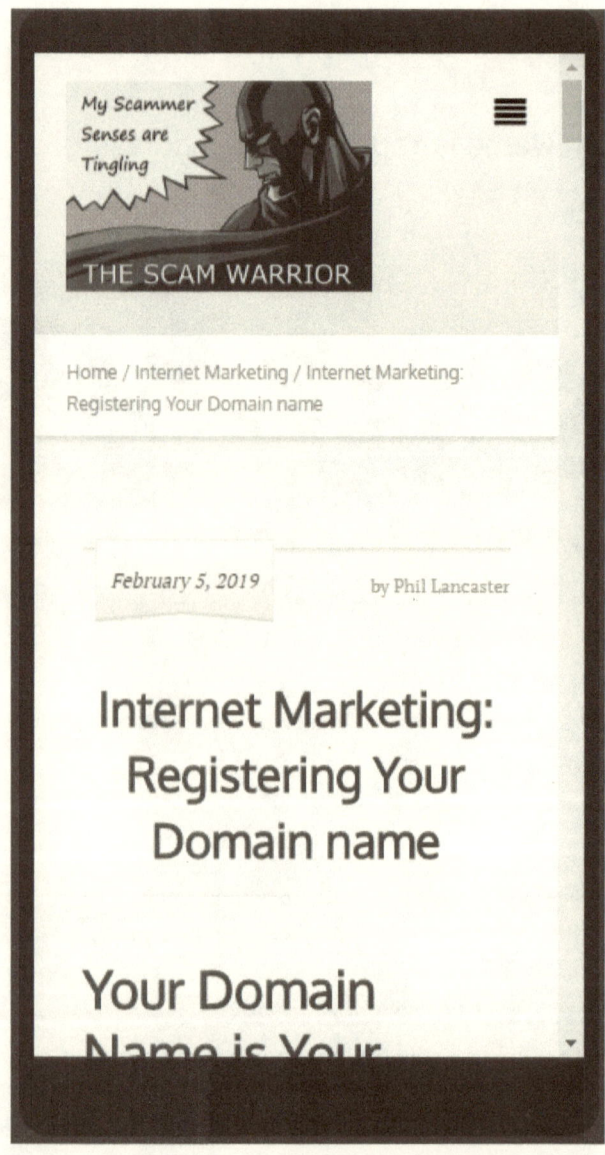

Figure 35: Smartphone View

Building Your Website

with Thrive Themes and Plugins

The Post List Element

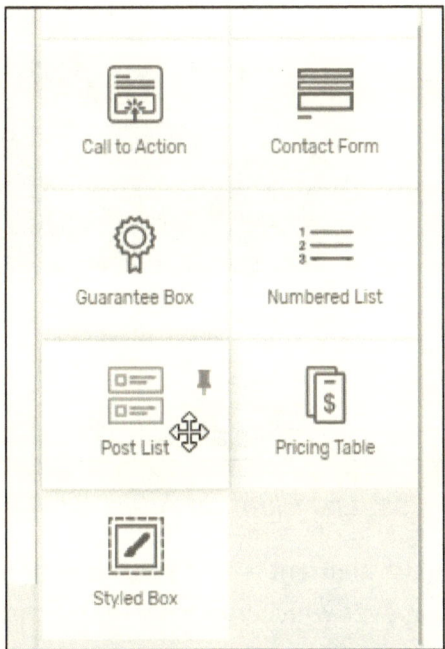

Figure 36: The Post List Element

The Post List element is incredibly powerful, delivering an impressive result for almost no work.

It can be used in many ways, but I'll give you one example and then you can experiment to get your own desired result.

I've created a new page called Articles and added it to my main menu.

The only thing on the page is a Post List element.

Building Your Website

with Thrive Themes and Plugins

Figure 37: Post List Element Added to Articles Page

The idea of the Post List element is to display any or all of your posts and pages in a grid pattern over which you have total control

I'm going to set mine up to display all posts in a 3 across grid, with the latest first, illustrated by the featured image, showing an excerpt and a Read More... tag.

The beauty is that once it's set up, new posts will automatically be added to it. No further attention is required.

Click on *Post List*, then *Edit Design*.

Building Your Website

with Thrive Themes and Plugins

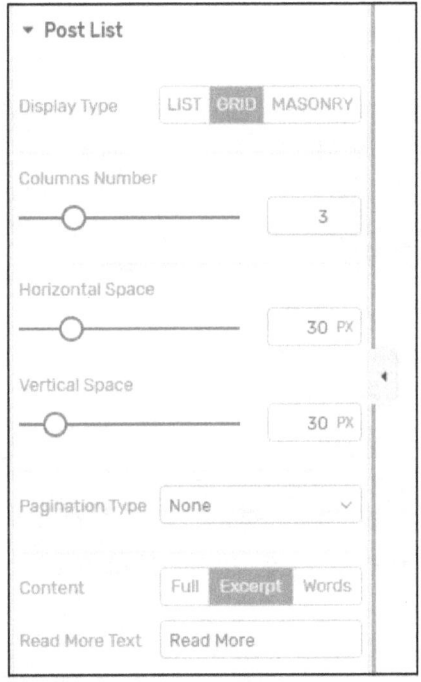

Figure 38: Post List Design

Here you can set:

Display Type	I use Grid
Number of Columns	I use 3
Content	I use Excerpt
Read More Text	I use "Read More"

Then click the **DONE** button.

Back under Post List, click Filter Posts.

Building Your Website

with Thrive Themes and Plugins

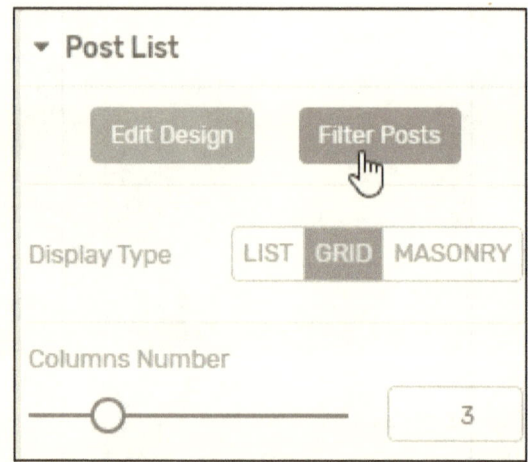

Figure 39: Filter Posts

Then set parameters for the posts to be displayed.

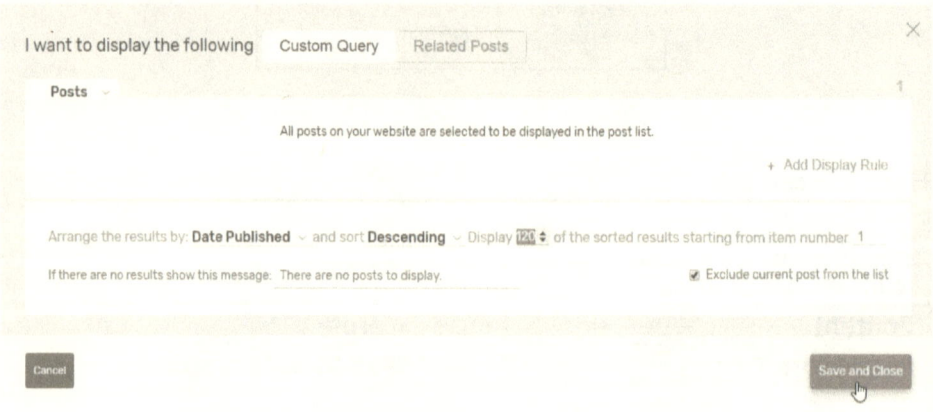

Figure 40: Select the Posts to be Displayed

If you simply want to display a large number of recent posts, set the number to be displayed and leave everything else.

Building Your Website

with Thrive Themes and Plugins

Figure 41: The Finished Articles Page

And that's it. With minimal work, I have a page that shows all my blog articles as soon as they're posted, nicely laid out and with a link to the full article.

Note that pages can be displayed in exactly the same manner. This can be an easy way of displaying groups of products by category.

Building Your Website

with Thrive Themes and Plugins

The Rest of the Books

Here are all the books in my Internet Marketing FAST series, all available as Kindle Singles.

Available Now

1. The 4 Things You Must Know (to Make Money While You Sleep)
2. How to Select Your Internet Marketing Niche
3. How to Register a Domain Name
4. How to Host Your Website
5. WordPress for the Technically Challenged
6. Building Your Website with Thrive
7. The Thrive User
8. The Thrive Expert

Not Yet Available

9. Become an Affiliate Marketing Ninja
10. Become an E-Commerce Ninja
11. The Deadly Combo of Blog Posts and Landing Pages
12. Google is Your New Best Friend
13. Building Your Mailing List
14. All About Free and Paid Traffic
15. How to Publish Your Book on Amazon
16. The Secret to Making Money with Your Internet Businesses (after You've Done Everything Else)

You can get the Kindle and Paperback links to the books on Amazon at

https://superaffiliatechallenge.com/internet-marketing-fast-books-from-amazon/

Building Your Website

with Thrive Themes and Plugins

About the Author

As an 80 year old (in 2024) fitness fanatic and successful internet marketer, Phil Lancaster is a bit of an anomaly.

Through a combination of bad luck and bad business decisions, he found himself broke and alone at 74.

Now, a few years later, he has several internet businesses that combine to bring him a 6-figure income.

It wasn't easy and he got burned a few times on the way, but he reckons that anyone can do it with the right road map.

He wants to help you to get started the way he did, but without making the same mistakes.

Anyone, from student to baby boomer (and older) can make money through the internet.

Phil's IM Fast series of mini-books will get you started. At just $2.99 each, you won't find a better investment.